D1716820

TAYLOR SWIFT

by K.C. Kelley

Consultant: Starshine Roshell
Music and Entertainment Journalist
Santa Barbara, CA

BEARPORT
PUBLISHING

New York, New York

Credits

Cover, © John Salangsang/Invision/AP Photo; 4, © EXImages/Alamy Stock Photo; 5, © John Shearer/LP5/Getty Images; 6, © Rick Diamond/Getty Images; 7, © Andrew Orth; 8L, Wikimedia Commons; 8–9, © Andrew Orth; 10, © Wikimedia Commons; 11, © AP Photo/Mark Humphrey; 12, © AP Photo/Mark Terrill; 13, © PA Images/Alamy Stock Photo; 14, © AP Photo/Robert Bukaty; 15, © AP Photo/Theron Kirkman; 16L, © WMTV/PacificCoastNews/ Newscom; 16–17, © Rex Features/via AP Images; 18L, © Everett Collection Inc./Alamy Stock Photo; 18–19, © ImagineChina/Newscom; 20, Wikimedia Commons; 21, © Hyperstar/Alamy Stock Photo; 22T, © AP Photo/ Mark Terrill; 22B, © Evgeny Karandaev/Shutterstock; 23T, © Phil McCarten/UPI/Newscom; 23B, © John Shearer/ LP5/Getty Images.

Publisher: Kenn Goin
Creative Director: Spencer Brinker
Production and Photo Research: Shoreline Publishing Group LLC

Library of Congress Cataloging-in-Publication Data

Names: Kelley, K. C., author.
Title: Taylor Swift / by K.C. Kelley.
Description: New York, New York : Bearport Publishing, [2018] | Series: Amazing Americans: pop music stars | Includes bibliographical references and index.
Identifiers: LCCN 2017045547 (print) | LCCN 2017045590 (ebook) | ISBN 9781684025145 (ebook) | ISBN 9781684024568 (library)
Subjects: LCSH: Swift, Taylor, 1989-–Juvenile literature. | Women country musicians—United States—Biography—Juvenile literature.
Classification: LCC ML3930.S989 (ebook) | LCC ML3930.S989 K45 2018 (print) | DDC 782.421642092 [B] —dc23
LC record available at https://lccn.loc.gov/2017045547

For more information, write to Bearport Publishing Company, Inc., 45 West 21st Street, Suite 3B, New York, New York 10010. Printed in the United States of America.

10 9 8 7 6 5 4 3 2 1

CONTENTS

Superstar!

It was September 2015 in Nashville, Tennessee. Taylor Swift had just begun her show at the Bridgestone Arena. Screams and shouts from fans filled the air. The whole city felt their excitement. After all, Nashville is where Taylor first became famous.

Taylor snaps a selfie with fans.

Six of Taylor's songs have become number-one hits.

Big Dreams

Taylor Alison Swift was born on December 13, 1989. Her family lived on a Christmas tree farm in Reading, Pennsylvania. Even when she was little, Taylor's parents saw her talent for singing and songwriting. When she was about twelve, Taylor took up the guitar. Soon, she dreamed of being a big star.

Taylor with her dad, Scott, and mom, Andrea

6

At the age of six, Taylor got her first country record. It was *Blue* by LeAnn Rimes.

7

To Nashville

When Taylor was fourteen, her family moved to Nashville, Tennessee—the heart of country music. In 2005, Taylor was performing at a local club called The Bluebird Cafe. A music **scout** saw her there and gave her a record **contract**!

Taylor played at this Nashville music club.

Taylor at age 14

Taylor's first single was "Tim McGraw." In 2006, it became a number-one hit!

Dreams Come True

Her first album, *Taylor Swift*, came out in 2006. Taylor was still in high school at the time. It was the best-selling country album of the year! Young girls were huge fans of Taylor's music. Her **lyrics** were about love and being a teenager.

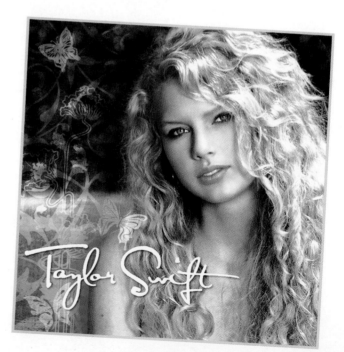

The cover of Taylor's first album

In 2007, Taylor made a short album of country Christmas songs. It was called *The Taylor Swift Holiday Collection*.

National Star

Taylor's second major album, called *Fearless*, came out in 2008. Taylor played songs from the album at numerous sold-out **concerts**. *Fearless* won Taylor a 2010 **Grammy** for Album of the Year!

Taylor won three other Grammys in 2010. One was for "White Horse" as Best Country Song.

Taylor performs songs from *Fearless* in England in 2009.

Worldwide Fame

Taylor became famous around the world. In 2010, she put out her third album, *Speak Now.* It sold more than one million copies in its first week! On the *Speak Now* Tour, she performed before huge crowds. Many performances were sold out!

Fans greet Taylor during the *Speak Now* Tour.

Taylor in Australia for her *Speak Now* Tour

Speak Now went **platinum**, which means it sold one million copies.

15

The Red Tour

In 2012, Taylor released *Red*, her fourth album. After it came out, Taylor started the *Red* Tour. She performed her songs for fans around the world. Taylor asked musical friends to join her on tour. Ed Sheeran, Rascal Flatts, and Luke Bryan came along!

Singer and songwriter Ed Sheeran

During the *Red* Tour, Taylor performed in 62 cities in 11 countries!

Music Mix

In 2014, Taylor tried a new style of music with her album *1989*. She had been making country music. Now she performed pop songs. Her fans didn't mind. They loved her new style, which made *1989* another number-one hit.

Taylor won Grammys for Album of the Year in 2010 and 2014.

Taylor and her dancers take a bow on the *1989* Tour.

More than Music

Taylor is still making music. In 2017, she put out a new album called *Reputation*. Her talent and hard work have inspired many young singers. "Just be yourself," she says. "There is no one better!"

Taylor has appeared in ads for clothing, shoes, and makeup.

Keds

BRAVE SPEAKS FROM THE HEART.

Taylor at the 2016 Grammys

Timeline

**Here are some key dates
in Taylor Swift's life.**

1980 — 1990 — 2000 — 2010 — 2020

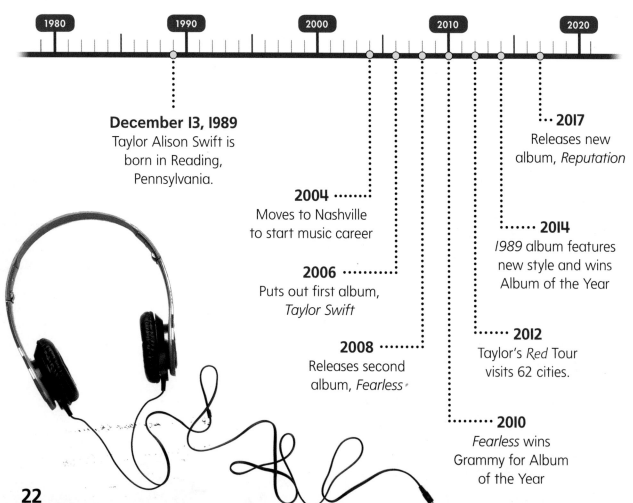

December 13, 1989
Taylor Alison Swift is
born in Reading,
Pennsylvania.

2004
Moves to Nashville
to start music career

2006
Puts out first album,
Taylor Swift

2008
Releases second
album, *Fearless*

2010
Fearless wins
Grammy for Album
of the Year

2012
Taylor's *Red* Tour
visits 62 cities.

2014
1989 album features
new style and wins
Album of the Year

2017
Releases new
album, *Reputation*

Glossary

concerts (KAHN-serts) performances of music in front of an audience

contract (KON-trakt) a written agreement between two people

Grammy (GRAMM-ee) an award given to musicians for the best music each year

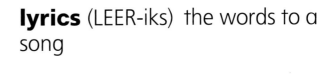

lyrics (LEER-iks) the words to a song

platinum (PLATT-ih-num) what a record album that sells one million or more copies is called

scout (SKOWT) a person who looks for future talent

Index

Read More

Brooks, Riley, and Molly Hodgin. *Taylor Swift: The Story of Me.* New York: Scholastic (2012).

Morreale, Marie. *Taylor Swift: Born to Sing (Rookie Biographies).* New York: Children's Press (2017).

Ryals, Lexi. *When I Grow Up: Taylor Swift.* New York, Scholastic (2015).

Learn More Online

To learn more about Taylor Swift, visit
www.bearportpublishing.com/AmazingAmericans

About the Author

K.C. Kelley has written more than 100 books for young readers on history, science, music, sports, nature, and other topics.